Rivers *of* Hope *a* Step by Step Approach *to* Dealing *with* Adversity

GENE ROBERTS

AuthorHouse™
1663 Liberty Drive
Bloomington, IN 47403
www.authorhouse.com
Phone: 1 (800) 839-8640

Because of the dynamic nature of the Internet, any web addresses or links contained in this book may have changed
since publication and may no longer be valid. The views expressed in this work are solely those of the author and do not
necessarily reflect the views of the publisher, and the publisher hereby disclaims any responsibility for them.

Any people depicted in stock imagery provided by Getty Images are models,
and such images are being used for illustrative purposes only.
Certain stock imagery © Getty Images.

This book is printed on acid-free paper.

KJV
Scripture taken from The Holy Bible, King James Version. Public Domain

NASB
Scripture quotations marked NASB are taken from the New American Standard Bible®, Copyright © 1960, 1962,
1963, 1968, 1971, 1972, 1973, 1975, 1977, 1995 by The Lockman Foundation. Used by permission.

NIV
Scripture quotations marked NIV are taken from the Holy Bible, New International Version®. NIV®. Copyright © 1973,
1978, 1984 by International Bible Society. Used by permission of Zondervan. All rights reserved. [Biblica]

NLT
Scripture quotations marked NLT are taken from the Holy Bible, New Living Translation, copyright © 1996, 2004, 2007.
Used by permission of Tyndale House Publishers, Inc. Carol Stream, Illinois 60188. All rights reserved. Website

ISBN: 978-1-7283-2828-7 (sc)
ISBN: 978-1-7283-2827-0 (e)

Library of Congress Control Number: 2019914922

Print information available on the last page.

Published by AuthorHouse 09/27/2019

author**HOUSE**®

Never give up.

Contents

Introduction vii

Chapter One   Who Is God (Yahweh, Yhwh)? 1

Chapter Two   Exploring The Old Testament 7

Chapter Three   A Man Named Yeshua (Jesus) 13

Chapter Four   Exploring The New Testament 19

Chapter Five   So, Why Do Christians Suffer? 25

Chapter Six   God Is Still In Charge 33

Chapter Seven   Hinderances To Prayer And Healing. 39

Chapter Eight   God Has And We Need An Open Accepting Heart. 45

Chapter Nine   Some Things I Still Do Not Understand. 51

Chapter Ten   My Journey. 57

Broken crayons still color.

We have all been broken at some point in our life… God loves us regardless…

Introduction

I read various statistics that indicate many people claim to be Christian. Somewhere between 80% and 90% of the U.S. Population claim to believe in God. Many of these people believe "doing good" will get them into Heaven. Many "preachers" will preach that same lie from the pulpit. I have also read only about 1/3 of the population believe hell is as an actual "real" place of eternal torment. Many, "preachers", if they even mention hell, may preach that same lie.

Another problem – many of the 80% to 90% of those who do believe in God are looking for their own way of fulfilling Mathew 6:33 (seek first the kingdom of God). They are not looking for "THE WAY".

We all have challenges. I determined several years ago I would not allow "problems" into my life. Challenges, yes. Problems, no. I would try my best to be as Paul … "content in whatever state he was in". Philippians 4:11 Some days I am even successful!!

I have been in health care for over 47 years. EMS (Emergency Medical Services), Nursing – ICU, ER and long term care. I have witnessed and been a part of much in the way of suffering. My personal list is pretty short compared to others.

So, why do Christians face adversity? Why do Christians suffer? Why do children, little children, suffer? Disease, cancer, sexual abuse, child abuse, abortion … Why doesn't God do something? Why doesn't God answer our prayers? Just who is this God anyway? (Just a positive note here: for someone who has had an abortion, there is forgiveness in the blood of the cross, in the blood of Yeshua {Jesus}).

My prayer is that by the time you reach the end of this short book, you will have a better understanding of some of the questions and even more so, an understanding of *the* answer. The intent is to keep this short and to the point. I do not even read long journal or magazine articles. I do not like thick books with long, rambling chapters. I certainly do not have all the answers and as some would say, I don't even know all the questions.

However, I do know the **One** who does have "*the answer*". If you do not know Him now, I pray you will by the time you finish reading this.

I have struggled at times to understand the whys and the why nots. I am becoming more and more convinced that understanding it all is less and less important. That is why we call it faith.

You will need a Bible. Many of the verses listed you will need to look up on your own. It is my belief that when you do so, the verses will "stick" in your mind and heart much better. Besides, if you do not have a Bible, you realllllllllly need to get one.

Chapter One

Who Is God (Yahweh, Yhwh)?

Key Verse: Exodus 3:14 I am that I am.

As mentioned, some 80% to 90% of the U.S. claim to believe in God. Some statistics show as many as 75% believe "to do good" will get you to Heaven. So why does America continue to deteriorate spiritually? Seems many folks feel this way. Are we still a Christian nation? Many would say no. So, who or what is this God so many claim to believe in? Let's explore some of what the Bible has to say about God.

Exodus 3:14 God says "I am that I am". (KJV) "I am who I am". (NIV) "I am the One who always is". (NLT)
I John 4:8 God is love. (NASB)
I John 1:5 God is Light. (NASB)
John 4:24 God is a spirit. (KJV) God is spirit. (NIV, NLT)
John 1:1 "... the Word was with God ... the word was God". (KJV)
John 1:14 "The Word was made flesh". (KJV) more later about Jesus or Yeshua.

This is just the beginning. Ann Spangler, in her book, "Praying the Names of God", lists 26 names or titles for God. This is an awesome book and a must for any library.

So, God has many names or titles: Yahweh (or YHWH), El, Elohim, Jehovah (maybe the most well known) to mention only a few. God has a name or title for many of His awesome powers or characteristics.

Let's look at some of those names or titles:

Elohim: Genesis 1:1, In the beginning, God (Elohim – Creator) created the heavens and the earth. (NIV) (See also KJV, Scofield Reference Bible notes). Even in todays world, if you make or create something, you have certain rights regarding whatever it is. As creator of the universe, God has the right and authority to oversee His creation as He desires. God made it. It is His. The universe is subject to God. Since He created us, we are subject to God. (See Spangler, Praying the names of God)

Yahweh Rophe: Healer (Praying the names of God, p98). Do you, or someone you know or love, have cancer, arthritis, heart disease, or any other of the number of ailments that befall humankind? Have you prayed and received healing? Praise the Lord. Have you prayed and not received healing? Praise the Lord anyway. (See Job 1:21,22, 13:15, 19:25). God is not only a healer, He is THE HEALER. (Exodus 15:26, Isaiah 53:5, 1 Peter 2:24) Don Moen puts this to a beautiful song in a truly awesome way with "I am the God that Healeth Thee". Why are some healed and some not healed? I do not know the answer to that, but I know THE ONE who does. The answers to that question are probably as many and as varied as the number of those who have asked. More on this subject in chapter four.

El Shaddai (or El Shaddy) God Almighty. See Genesis 17:1. (See also NASB notes). Webster defines almighty as "all powerful". All is defined as "wholly, entirely, totality, the whole extent, the greatest possible, every part or bit …" Starting to get the picture? One of my favorite little sayings is "the same thing only different". So, Elohim and Shaddai are the same God, just different titles. Sandi Patty sings an awesome song of El Shaddai.

Abba (Spangler, Praying the Names of God, P. 319) This is one my favorites for God. It may be translated as Father, but my favorite translation is "Daddy". You can usually recognize someone with Southern Heritage. Adult women (especially) and often adult men will use "daddy" when referring to their father. On a pillow given to me by one of my daughters; "Any man can be a father, it takes someone special to be a Dad." (daddy)

Yahweh Shalom: Shalom is translated and means "peace". It means so much more. "...Shalom actually incorporates all the elements that go into making a God centered community – peace, prosperity, rest, safety, security, justice, happiness, health, welfare, wholeness." (Shelly and Miller, Called to Care, p 167). Yet the Apostle Paul was content in prison (Philippians 4:11). Shalom – Peace? He knew God was in charge, so Shalom? Probably. He did not have all of those things listed, at least not physically while in prison, but he knew they were coming. Shalom – YES!

Using different names or titles is actually common practice. My "legal" name is Marion Eugene Roberts. The first 10 or so years of my life I was called or known by Eugene. The last 60 or so years I have used Gene. As I have become older, I often use Marion. I am also a father, dad, daddy, gramps, grandpa, pa pa, brother, son, husband, nurse, paramedic, friend …

God has more than one name, title, power, attribute, description, etc.. While many may feel translating most of those differences to simply God, Lord, Lord God, etc., has made the Bible easier to read, we have lost sight of just who God is. The use of the name Jehovah is actually fairly recent in history. The name Jehovah was first used in the middle ages and enshrined in the King James Version of the Bible. (Praying the Names of God, p77). Spangler gives a good explanation as to why and how this came to be. I am still not sure how you can make up a new name for the God of the universe. This just really bothers me, but I may well be in the minority of one!

I personally wish the translators would have left the names in their original form. Many books, authors and pastors do use the original Yahweh when referring to God and Yeshua when referring to Jesus. I just know after reading Spangler's books, "Praying the Names of God" and Praying the Names of Jesus", I had a much better grasp of their Biblical picture. I am now more careful in reading both new and old testaments. I am more careful in trying to understand what difference it might make when different names or titles are used. And I often read more than one translation. The "Parallel Bible" by Zondervan has been a helpful tool and includes King James, NASB, NIV and NLT. Notes in the Scofield Bible have also proven helpful.

Regardless of name or title, I have heard time and again, what makes God so awesome is not the fact He created the universe, but that He knows me, cares for me and desires a personal relationship with me. As a believer (born again Christian) my name is written on the palm of His hand (Isaiah 49:16).

The end result however is very simple. God is who / what He said. "I am that I am". And there is no other (Isaiah 45:18). (I still like Abba {Daddy}).

Chapter Two

Exploring The Old Testament

**Key Verse: Genesis 1:31 And God saw everything
He had made, and behold,
it was very good. (KJV)**

For a short time the world was without sin. No mention of death, disease, suffering or even the dreaded four letter word … "work". Adam and Eve "tended" the garden. (NLT). The KJV says "dress and keep". As we see from Genesis 1:31, the creation, including man, was "very good".

All would soon change. God warned Adam and Eve they would die if they ate from the tree of knowledge. How or when they would die was not explained. Violence and death was soon a part of this world as we know from the story of Cain and Able (Genesis 4:8). Able actually received favor from God for his offering and his "reward" was to be killed by his brother. The Old Testament has several stories where things did not go well for God's chosen or favored. Genesis chapters 37 through 41 tell the story of Joseph. Even though he was sold by his brothers and endured adversity for a time, he remained faithful. And then Job. How many of us could endure what Job went through? Yet he continued to trust God (Job 13:15). Many have tried to say Job is "just a story". That Job did not really exist. The Bible is God's word, cover to cover. Why then is Job even mentioned and especially in such a detailed story? As an example? A parable? Many, if not most believe Job to be an actual true story. Ezekiel (14:20) and James (5:11) both make mention of Job.

David: David was in an adulterous affair with Bathsheba. He killed her husband Uriah, who by the way was totally committed to King David. David did not "pull the trigger", but that is only a technicality. (see II Samuel chapter 11). Even with these circumstances, David knew his salvation was still secure. (II Samuel 12:23). Their first son died. (chapter 12). I have experienced the death of a grandchild. I, like David, know the future and that I will eventually see him in Heaven. However, 30 some years later the pain is still very real. II Samuel chapters 13 and 15 tell how David's sons turned against him. Was this the result of the sins David had committed? Maybe. I leave that to the more scholarly. What I do know and what the Bible says is this: Before any of this occurred. Samuel anointed David with oil and "the Spirit of the Lord came upon him (David) from that day forward."

(I Samuel 16:13). Psalm 51 is David's prayer of repentance.

Sometimes our pain, problems or suffering may be "self imposed". That is, we often cause our own problems. Jonah spent 3 days and 3 nights in the belly of a great fish. Why? Because of disobedience. (Jonah 1:17). Some will claim the story of Jonah cannot be true. If God can create the entire universe (and He did), He can certainly put someone in the belly of a great fish.

God's plan, God's answer is not always what we think we want. Or, I think that won't work, so I will try it my way. Or, I try my way before I even ask God for guidance. Would I have stood with Shadrack, Meshack and Abednego who were willing to die? (Daniel chapter 3). As was Daniel. (Daniel chapter 6).

Does God send the storm, or simply allow the storm? Sometimes we cause our own storm. Jonah, David, the Israelites in 40 years of wandering in the desert. I am sure there are more, but you get the point. But what about Able, Joseph, Job? Able went to Heaven. Joseph was tested for a reason as was Job. God used the test for later greatness.

Remember Genesis 1:31? All of creation, at one point, was "very good". Then came sin (Genesis 3:6). Sin is a word, term or subject that seems to be mentioned very little these days, even in some churches. Preachers preach the world instead of the Word. Many are looking for what sounds good to their "itching ears". (II Timothy 4:3). The Israelites did not want to hear from Caleb and Joshua. (Numbers chapters 13 and 14). God had already given them the land of Canaan. (Numbers 13.2). IT WAS THEIRS FOR THE TAKING!! (emphasis mine). But what happened? Fear, uncertainty, lack of faith. They paid a price.

Why are we here? Many have asked, few seem to care. What is our purpose? Few seem to care. Our duty, purpose, or whatever you want to call it is: "Fear (Love) God and keep His commandments, for this is the whole duty of man. (Ecclesiastes 12:13) KJV. Will this make our lives pain free, sorrow free, problem free, challenge free? No. But our actions will follow us into eternity. Ecclesiastes 12:14, "For God shall bring every work into judgment, with every secret thing, whether it be good or whether it be evil." I am not sure how it can be put any more clearly. We will find out later, in "Exploring the New Testament", that God not only forgives sin, but God also forgets forgiven sin. It would seem here He is speaking about or to the lost. Pain, suffering and death came upon humankind soon after creation. Christian suffering occurred in the time of Jesus and it continues today, many giving their lives in maintaining their faith.

Is the Old Testament just a history lesson? Are God's promises still the same today? "IF", the Jesus of the New Testament is the same God of the Old Testament (John 1:1 and 1:14, Colossians 1:16) and "IF" He is the same yesterday, today and forever (Hebrews 13:8), then His promises are most certainly still the same for today. Then we should still apply Ecclesiastes 12:13.

It can be easy to forget "our duty", especially when things are not going well. Job did not forget. David was on quite a roller coaster of cries for help and of praises for blessings. Many times in Psalms, David cries out to God for help and to "hurry". (Psalm 22:19, 38:22, 40:13, 70:1, 71:12). In all of the pain and suffering, God was still with His chosen. Caleb and Joshua, David, Jonah, Joseph, Job. In obedience and even in disobedience. Whether

God sends the storm or just allows the storm, He is still God, He is still with us and He is still in the miracle working business. From a burning bush (Genesis 3) to a parting of the waters (Exodus 14:21) to Yeshua's healings (some 30+ in the New Testament), to healings and miracles of today. He is a God of miracles, truth and justice.

God does have a plan for us (Jeremiah 29:11). We are obviously the ones who often disrupt His plan. You have probably heard someone say "I am working on plan B or plan C". I am not sure how far down the alphabet God has gone with me, but I am sure it is much further than He should have. Glory be to God, when I have messed up, He has not left me. When I (finally) come to my senses and ask forgiveness and ask for His help, He has ALWAYS been there. I have often heard, "When God closes one door, He always opens another ... even though sometimes it is hell in the hallway!" I believe I have spent some time in the hallway – and yes, my choices put me there. Some will still say the Old Testament no longer applies or specific verses are for a specific time. If you do not believe II Chronicles 7:14 applies to America today, you may as well just stop here and not go on.

Chapter Three

A Man Named Yeshua (Jesus)

Key Verse: John 8:58
…before Abraham was, I am.

Yeshua or Jesus is as old as the Old Testament. I believe He was introduced in Genesis 1:26. "And God said, let "US" make man in "OUR" image. (emphasis and quotes mine) To whom was God speaking? Who is the us and who is the our? The answer I believe is Yeshua. (note: Yeshua is the Hebrew name for Jesus).

The book of John pretty much tells us how Jesus fits in the God Head. John 1:1, "In the beginning was the Word and the Word was with God and the Word was God." John 1:3, "All things were made by Him; and without Him was not anything made that was made." John 1:14, "And the Word was made flesh and dwelt among us." Colossians 1:16 adds "For by Him were all things created." (all KJV).

Now with or without rocket science, some pretty basic facts are made clear. There was (still is) the Word. The Word (someone / something) was with God. The Word was (still is) God. And the Word became flesh. Yeshua (Jesus). See again the key verse, "... before Abraham was, I am." (see Exodus 3:14 reference to "I am"). Ephesians 3:9 states "... God, who created all things by Jesus Christ." See also John 1:3, Colossians 1:16, Hebrews 1:2.

Jesus said "... he that hath seen me hath seen the Father." John 14:9. (all references KJV). Jesus is 100% human flesh. Jesus is 100% God. Maybe you already knew that?

What else might we learn about this Jesus? His name means Yahweh saves or Yahweh is salvation. (Names of Jesus, Spangler, p. 85). Much like YHWH, Yahweh and Jehovah are names of God, the name Jesus has a bit of transition as well. Go back to Numbers 13:8 and we find reference to a man Oshea (KJV) or Hoshea (NIV, NASB, NLT). Depending on the translation used, his name became Jehoshua (and later Joshua) which means Savior or the Lord is salvation. (Scofield Reference Bible). Jesus is a form of Joshua or Yehoshua. The Hebrew for Jesus is Yeshua. (my personal preference).

See "Names of Jesus" by Spangler. See also "Today's Parallel Bible" (Zondervan, pp332, 333). Let's explore some more of what the Bible has to say about this Jesus or Yeshua:
Most everyone is familiar with John 3:16, For God so loved the world ....
John 10:30 Jesus said He and the Father are one ...
John 14:6 No man comes to the Father but by Him. (Jesus)
John 14:9 If you have seen Me, you have seen the Father. (Jesus speaking)
Matthew 1:23 He is Emmanuel, God with us.
Luke 1:32 Son of David.
Luke 1:35 Son of God.
Matthew 20:28, 26:64 Son of man.
John 1:29 Lamb of God.
Revelation 22:13 Alpha and Omega.
John 13:3-8, 12:17 Rabbi / Teacher
Matthew 16:16, John 4:25 Christ / Messiah
Philippians 2:9-11 He is Lord.
Matthew 1:22, 20:28, Luke 22:27, Philippians 2:7 Came to serve.
Matthew 4:1, Mark 1:13, Luke 4:2, Hebrews 2:18, 4:15 He was tempted.
Mark 8:31, 9:12, Luke 9:22, 17:25 He came to suffer.
John 5:20 The Father judges no man. He has committed all judgment to the Son.

As for a personal relationship with Jesus Christ, we have several promises from scripture. Jesus is our advocate, John 2:1. Jesus is at the right hand of God "making intercession for us", Romans 8:34 (KJV). (… "pleading" for us. NLT). And Romans 8:26 tells us "... the Spirit Itself maketh intercession for us with groanings which cannot be uttered"(KJV), or "groans that words cannot express" (NIV). And verse 27, "... the Spirit pleads for us believers ...", NLT, or "... intercedes for the saints according to the will of God." NASB. A thought from a late church sister, Bwana Drennan, was Satan cannot understand the "groanings", does not know what the Holy Spirit is saying and therefore is unable to interfere. Jesus AND the Holy Spirit interceding and PLEADING for me and you. That is almost beyond my comprehension.

A few words specifically related to salvation. How can we be assured of a relationship with Jesus?

Do you need to be saved? Just what does that mean? What does it take to get to Heaven? Well, let's see what the Bible says.

Romans 3:10 says "There is none righteous, no not one." Romans 3:23 adds "For all have sinned and come short of the glory of God. Romans 6:23 tells us the penalty, "For the wages of sin is death; but the gift of God is eternal life through Jesus Christ our Lord." John 3:16 is probably the first verse most Christians learn as the solution to sin. "For God so loved the world, that He gave His only begotten Son, that whosoever believeth in Him should not perish, but have everlasting life."

So how does all this believing take place and what does it mean? Jesus was crucified and died for our sins. See I Corinthians 1:23 and 2:2. Jesus was raised from the dead, Romans 6:4. So then when we believe, see Romans 10:9, "... if thou shalt confess with thy mouth the Lord Jesus, and shalt believe in thine heart that God raised him from the dead, thou shalt be saved." Ephesians 2:8, 9 tell us we cannot work our way into heaven. It is a free gift. I John 1:9 assures us of forgiveness. "If we confess our sins, He is fatiful and just to forgive us our sins, and to cleanse us from all unrighteousness.

Once we are saved, the Bible then has multiple verses to let us know we can never lose our salvation. Here is part of John 10:27-30. Verse 28, "And I give unto them eternal life; and they shall never perish, neither shall any man pluck them out of my hand." Parts of Romans 8:34-39. Verse 34, (Jesus) "... who is at the right hand of God, who also maketh intercession for us." Verses 38, 39, "For I (Paul) am persuaded that neither death, nor life, nor angels, nor principalities, nor powers ... nor height, nor depth, nor any other creature shall be able to separate us from the love of God..." I Corinthians 1:7,8, "who shall confirm you unto the end, that ye may be found blameless in day of our Lord Jesus Christ." Ephesians 4:30, "... ye are sealed unto the day of redemption." Jude verse 24, "... unto Him that is able to keep you from falling, and to present you faultless..."

Yes, once saved, you are secure in the arms of Jesus from that day forward.

Chapter Four

Exploring The New Testament

**Key verse: John 15:7 If ye abide in Me and My words
in you, you shall ask what ye will and it shall be done
unto you.**

The world is full of sin, disease and death. Since Genesis there has been no escape. After "the fall" all of this and more is part of life. Jesus would "use" all of these as part of His ministry. In just two chapters of Matthew, chapters 8 and 9, there are 11 miracles. Most are healing, one is casting out a devil and in chapter 9, verse 2, Jesus openly forgave sin. In John chapter 11, Lazarus is raised from the dead. Someone smarter than me and with more patience, counted 33 healings in the New Testament.

One thing that has intrigued me and even baffled me; why did Jesus weep related to the Lazarus story?

He was late getting there. Most likely on purpose. Jesus already knew Lazarus was dead and He knew that He was going to raise him from the dead. IF that thought is still with me when I get to Heaven, I may ask Jesus about it in a couple thousand years!

The New Testament, much like the Old Testament, is full of promise and hope, mixed with trial and tribulation. Many healings and miracles as noted, mixed with death and martyrdom beginning with Stephan. We know Jesus sits at the right hand of God (Mark 16:19). And we know Jesus stood when Stephan was stoned (Acts 7:55). He may well stand for each martyr even today?

There may be times when reading the New Testament one would wonder why become a Christian. Stephan was stoned. Christians were persecuted, suffered and died. Most of the Apostles died a martyrs death. What of the miracles, the healings, the promises? I have heard it asked, who would doubt that if Jesus would walk into a funeral service today and take the hand of the dead and say arise – that person WOULD arise! Any and all whom he touched would be healed (and anyone who touched Him. {Luke 8}). Where are the miracles, the healings, the promises? Why the suffering? And all for His name. Why would I want to become a Christian? Well, here we go – let's look at just a few reasons …

By His stripes we are healed – Isaiah 53:5, I Peter 2:24.
If we ask anything according to His will, He will hear us – I John 5:14
James 5:13-15 gives us instruction for healing. Call the Elders together, pray over him or her and anoint with oil.
Key verse again: If ye abide in Me and My words in you, ye shall ask what ye will and it shall be done unto you. John 15:7. There are conditions for this one.
John 14: 13 Whatsoever you ask in My name, that I will do. Would include the same conditions.
Jesus tells us in Luke 8:48 and Luke 18:42, faith is the key.
John 3:16 pretty much sums it up - whosoever believes in Him would not perish, but have *eternal life,* (in Heaven). That is reason enough!!
James 4:3 however, gives us a reason why we do not receive. We ask "amiss". Give that one some thought.

God already knows our "wants", desires and NEEDS (Matthew 6:8 and 32). God knows every day, every minute of and about our life. David writes in Psalms 139:16, "You saw me before I was born. Every day of my life was recorded in your book, every moment was laid out before a single day had passed" (NLT). Jeremiah 1:5 confirms again, "Before I formed thee in the belly, I knew thee..." (KJV). And again from Matthew (above) we know God already knows our needs before we ask.

Whether we are healed of some disease or whether some "storm" is taken away or not is solely God's choice. Paul was not spared the "thorn in his side" and was in fact told God's grace would be sufficient. (II Corinthians 12:8,9). In Philippians 4:11, Paul wrote he was content in whatever state he was in. He was often in prison and he was not healed of his "thorn". Two verses later (verse 13) he boldly proclaimed he could do ANYTHING through Christ.

Jesus Himself set the example. Stephan followed. The apostles followed. Yet Paul also proclaimed "The sufferings of this time are not worthy to be compared with the glory which shall be revealed in us. (Romans 8:18 KJV). I Corinthians 2:9 puts it this way "... eye hath not seen, nor ear heard, neither have entered into the heart of man, the things which God hath prepared for them that love Him (KJV). The "Roberts version" ... not in my wildest dreams or imagination could I even come close to what Heaven will be!! Yes, that is reason enough for me!

It would seem we all want to be healed or blessed. So, we say a prayer, are not healed or blessed the way we wanted, give up in unbelief, continue on with a huge scar on our heart and what little faith we have left. I have heard pastors describe this kind of faith many different ways. One that stuck in my mind and heart is "crisis oriented Christianity". We want a miracle, a "parting of the waters" for every challenge, problem or crisis we encounter. Then, when we do not get what we want or get our way, we begin to doubt.

We are told where two or three are gathered in His name, He is there. (Matthew 18:20). Wow, for real? YES! Jesus said it, but do we really believe it? Have you ever been in a situation where you were seeking the Lord and have a "warm tingling" all over you? Or have a "chill" run down your spine? Or to be so overwhelmed with "a feeling" you actually thought you might faint or wondered if that really was a glimpse of Heaven or a glimpse of Jesus? That has not happened often or routinely, but I have "been there". It is something you cannot put into words or something you will ever forget.

Jesus tells us with faith as a grain of mustard seed, "WE" can move mountains. Nothing shall be impossible. (Matthew 17:20). Whatever we ask in prayer, believing, we will receive. (Matthew 21:22).

How does this all come about? Prayer and fasting. (Matthew 17:21). OK. I say a prayer, give up a burger and fries and … nothing happens. But wait. I will do what James said (5:14). Have the elders pray, anointing with oil, in the name of the Lord and … nothing happens. Well, go back a couple of pages. Re-read John 14:13 and 14, I John 5:14 and John 15:7. We MUST abide in Him and His words MUST abide in us. More on this later in chapter7.

Yes, God already knows what we "need" before we ask. (Matthew 6:8). So why ask? OK, OK. I will say the Lord's Prayer. Reciting the Lord's Prayer is OK. But Jesus gave this as an example, not a cure all. There are however, several points in this example. We need to "learn how to pray". "The effectual, fervent prayer of a righteous man availeth much" (James 5:16b). Someone came up with a way to develop a "way to pray". Use the word "ACTS". This has worked well for me and I keep it next to my bed. A- Adoration or praise to and for God. C- Confession of sin. (Even born again Christians do sin ya know!) T- Thanksgiving for what God has already provided and for what He is going to provide. S- Supplication. We are told to come humbly yet boldly before the throne. (Hebrews 4:16). Humbly as (forgiven) <u>sinners</u>, yet boldly as <u>forgiven</u> (sinners), <u>expecting</u> an answer. I am sure there are many other ways to pray, but ACTS has worked well for me. Still, reciting a prayer or praying in certain way for a certain thing does not always "part the water". (And no – I do not believe hitting "like" and typing "Amen" on face book will get you anywhere or anything!)

Few would doubt Paul had as much or more faith than anyone. Yet he was not healed or delivered from the "thorn in the flesh" (a messenger from satan). (II Corinthians 12:7-10). Paul however did not waiver. He actually took strength and glory through Christ in his infirmities. Infirmities and prison could not shake him (Philippians 4:11) boldly stating (verse 13) he could do all things through Christ.

Then there is John 15:7 again. The key verse for this chapter. I am not judging – just asking. How many of us actually "abide in Christ" on a "full time" basis? 24/7, all day, every day, without fail, without faltering? I do not know about you, but I am afraid I would have to say no. See again, Colossians 3:16 and I John 2:13-17.

And then I am reminded of I Corinthians 2:9; … eye hath not seen, nor ear heard, neither have entered into the heart of man, the things which God hath prepared for them that love Him.

Chapter Five

So, Why Do Christians Suffer?

**Key verse: I Peter 4:12 … think it not strange the
fiery trial which is to try you …**

As with any of the key verses listed, there may be several other verses just as applicable. The verse in I Peter is just one example of warnings about suffering. Continue reading verses 13,14 and 16 and then check the references for those verses. We are told to rejoice. We should rejoice when we are reproached for the name of Christ. People keep asking why is there so much suffering, why Christians suffer. Where was God on 9/11? Where was God at Columbine? Where was God at Newtown? Rest assured, God was at every one of those places. There has been some discussion about suffering in previous chapters, but we will look much closer in the next few pages.

The lesson of suffering is not an easy one. Years ago I did not understand. Today, at times, maybe I am still not so sure. But I do not ask why or why not anymore. If I did question anything, it would most likely be "God (Yahweh), Jesus (Yeshua), why do you, how can you love me so much? That, I may never understand.

This chapter is not to say Christians cannot or will not be blessed or become wealthy here on earth. I will just take you back to the verses above and some we have already mentioned and a few more to come. The trip here on earth may be bumpy, even tortuous and maybe even "fatal". Well, unless we are alive at the rapture, all of us will die … some much earlier than others. The destination for the born again Christian (Heaven) will be worth whatever we may face down here (Romans 8:18). Fatal is in italics for a reason. Though we may die here, of whatever cause, we will enter eternal life with Jesus.

We actually should expect a bumpy road with hindrances, challenges and suffering. We are told in I Peter 4:12 be not surprised (NASB) for a testing … to share in Christ's sufferings. We are also told to rejoice in verse 13. Only a soul totally committed to Christ can begin to understand this. I Peter 1:7 tells us trials are to show our faith strong and pure (NLT). James 1:2 tells us to count it pure joy (NIV).

See Acts 5:40 and 41. The apostles were beaten and they departed REJOICING (emphasis mine) that they were counted worthy to suffer for Jesus.

"Faith that triumphantly soars is possible only when the winds of life are contrary to personal comfort. That kind of faith is His ultimate purpose in allowing us to encounter storms of suffering". Ann Graham Lotz in the book "Why" (W Publishing, 2004).

There may be times when we suffer so we can be an instrument for others who suffer or will suffer similar circumstances. See II Corinthians 1:4. Someone who has never experienced cancer, the death of a child or grandchild would have a challenge trying to comfort someone with that challenge. Even pastors and counselors would have a hard time relating. We are taught in health care to NEVER say "I understand". Because we do not understand. I am NOT that person and I do NOT understand. Even if it is the same or similar situation, I am not that person with the same background, faith, thoughts, etc.. I can empathize with that person, but that is it. Still having been through a similar situation, I can share the pain and possibly some insight(s) which were helpful to me and may well help that person. Maybe you are being prepared for a situation in the future, that is someone elses future. Maybe God's grace actually will be sufficient. (Hmmmmmmm)

Be careful of preachers, commentaries, articles, books … be careful of this book! Prove all things.

(I Thessalonians 5:21). Be careful of those who "preach" that when you are sick and you are not healed it is from lack of faith. Be careful of those who say if you are not blessed financially or you suffer or you are lacking in something, that it is because of your lack of faith. See I John 4:1.

There will be, are, many false prophets. And there are many very wealthy ones on TV. Be careful … be very careful. This type of "preacher" has been labeled by some as a "new millennium Pharisee".

Harsh? Could be. Could be that it is true. Look at some more scripture warnings. "Having a form of Godliness, but denying the power thereof. (II Timothy 3:5 KJV). "Ever learning and never able to come to the knowledge of truth". (II Timothy 3:7). "They honor Him with their mouth and lips, but not their heart. They teach for doctrine the commandments of men" (Matthew 15:8,9). They will have itching ears, hearing what they want to hear. (II Timothy 4:3). There will be those who have prophesied, cast out devils and done many miracles, yet Jesus will say He never knew them. (Matthew 7:21-23).

Back to the why or why not of Christian suffering. We can start early in the Bible when Cain killed his brother Able (Genesis 4:8). Read the book of Job. He did nothing! Yet God gave him over to Satan; Job 1:11,12 and 2:6. The New Testament talks about chastening, Hebrews 12:5-11. But chastening is totally different and had nothing to do with Able or Job. Jeremiah 29:11 tells us God has thoughts or a plan of peace, not evil for us. Yet we are told to rejoice and have joy in suffering and temptation. See:

I Peter 4:12-14 we are told to rejoice.
Matthew 5:11,12 we are told we are blessed and told to rejoice.
Matthew 10:22 we will be hated.
James 1:2 told to count it joy.
Acts 16:23-25 Paul and Silas prayed and sang praises.

John 16:33 Jesus Himself warning us of tribulation.

II Corinthians 4:16-18 affliction works an eternal glory.

Just one more. Actually 3 in 1. Revelation 3:19 speaks of chastening. 3:20 gives us an opportunity to respond positively. 3:21 tells us our reward.

I am sure there are plenty more, but this should keep you busy for awhile. And yes, you obviously need a bible and if you want the full effect, you will need to look up the verses for yourself. (I find that extremely helpful). Hebrews 13:5 tells us Jesus will never leave us or forsake us. Some would argue "look at all the suffering in His name". I would argue "look at the end result – Heaven." "The experience of (suffering) loss itself does not have to be the defining moment of our lives. Instead, the defining moment can be our response to the loss." From Jerry Sittser, "When Your Rope Breaks" (Zondervan 2009).

Still not into suffering for His sake? Still prefer the name it and claim it group? Jesus Himself said it is easier for a camel to go through the eye of a needle than for a rich man to enter Heaven. (Matthew 19:24). Read Job again. The book of Psalms is a roller coaster of anguish and praise. Much, or at least some, of David's anguish (suffering) was his own fault. Let's see, there was Bathsheba, Uriah …

Jeremiah had this warning in chapter 2, verse 19, "Thine own wickedness shall correct thee and thy back slidings shall reprove thee ..." Habakkuk knew where to find joy, even when there was little or nothing to be joyful about. Habakkuk 3:17, "Although the fig tree shall not blossom … and there be no herd in the stall: vs 18, Yet will I rejoice in the Lord, I will joy in the God of my salvation."

The list of self made challenges is almost endless. Simple things like food, smoking, stress, exercise or lack of exercise can be the underlying cause of multiple medical problems. Gambling … many go bankrupt because of gambling. Alcohol … anything from spousal and child abuse to fatality accidents. It is the lack of control for many issues. The sex industry. How many marriages have gone by the wayside because of affairs or the sex industry? Management of finances? (Ouch!) We are, I am (probably still) poor steward(s) of what God has provided.

We live in America. Though often compromised, "they" haven't (yet) taken away our freedom of worship. Although many Christian owned businesses are losing the battle by being sued for not providing services for gays. There are stories on a regular basis about how "they" are trying to chew away Christian rights, literally one bite at a time. You can check at any of the following web sites to see just what I am referring to: American Family Association (AFA), Faith Family America, Jay Sekulow, Rutherford Institute, Alliance Defending Freedom (ADF), American Center for Law and Justice (ACLJ). Much blood has been shed for freedoms we often seem to take for granted. And whether you agree with war or not, much blood is at risk of being spilled yet today. I can still remember Tienanmen Square in China. 1989. A young man, run over by a tank, because he wanted just a taste of what we have. He lost. The people of China lost. And today, how much "stuff" do we buy that is made in China? It makes me sick to my stomach. How many Christians die every day in countries like China, Indonesia, North Korea, the middle east? Point is, we in America do not know what suffering is. We have little or no idea about Christian persecution. And we buy their stuff. More like garbage. And then we wonder why there is a lack of jobs in the U.S.. American's out of work for weeks, months, years. Sorry about the "soap box" … on second thought, no I am not sorry. Just think about it for awhile …

Suffering. What does it mean to suffer? There are probably as many thoughts about suffering as there are people suffering. From finances to actual persecution for Christian beliefs. My story is pretty tame compared to some. And yes, suffering comes in many ways. Many are taken to be with Jesus at an early age. From a few minutes or few hours to only a few years old. Others live into their 90's or more. Disease, accidents. I guess I do wonder sometimes. Especially about the young children. And maybe even the elderly. I have cared for many with Alzheimer's disease and some linger for years. I also know from various sources there has been and still is child sacrifice. Amazing … they cannot argue or fight back. Infantcide is practiced today without hesitation in many areas. Abortion. God knows us in the womb and actually before we are in the womb. (Jeremiah 1:5). How can that not be murder?

There is a positive afterthought about abortion or any sin for that matter. The afterthought is forgiveness. Forgiveness through the blood of Jesus Christ. Another afterthought from that is forgiven sin is forgotten sin. Hebrews 8:12, Hebrews 10:17, Isaiah 43:25, Psalm 103:12. God does not remember! So neither should we. (Easier said than done). You do not need to travel that road alone. Jesus will carry you. (poem "Footprints").

Yes, many will die young. Many will grow old and die. That is just the way it is. As a nurse, I have cared for many over 100 years old. But why so many at an early age? As a nurse and a paramedic I saw many children die. I do not know that it matters why. God is still in charge regardless of the circumstances. If we can understand that, then the whys will not matter as much.

So, what of the promises of Jesus? "... whatsoever ye ask in my name, that I will do ... If ye shall ask anything in my name, I will do it." John 14:13, 14 tells us He will do it. I John 5:14 may shed a little light on the issue. "If ye ask anything according to His will, He heareth us." Then look up James 4:2,3 again. Something about asking amiss.

Before becoming too absorbed in the promises, let's look at a few warnings, directly from Jesus. Matthew chapter 10. Over half of the chapter is related to suffering for His sake. Matthew chapter 24 tells of the beginning of sorrows for Christians. Christians have suffered since the time of Jesus. Jesus Himself tells us it will only get worse. We in America have no idea what Christian suffering is all about. Some believe when America is faced with true Christian persecution, many will not be ready for the challenges. Professing Christians verses true Christians? Only Jesus knows for sure. In the book "If You Are Going Through Hell, Keep Going" author Doug Giles tells us being a Christian is brutal. "If you are in a bad situation and you are thinking God is not going to come through for me, ... guess what; God is NOT going to come through for you!" (Pretty simple).

"By placing our suffering in the Lord's hands, we are saying, 'God, I cannot fix this. I am helpless. I am totally dependent on you.' This act of surrender releases God to do whatever He pleases in us and for us in our suffering." Ruth Graham, "When Your Rope Breaks", Zondervan 2009.

As mentioned, hardly a week goes by that a Christian group or school or business somewhere is being denied their Constitutional rights. Christmas is prime time but it is happening more often and anytime of the year. Anyone who can read and think for themselves knows there is NO such thing as "separation of church and state". The Constitution DOES prohibit laws that attack our freedom of religion. Seems the ACLU and liberal judges do not understand that. "They" are good at scaring people and at winning cases in liberal courts. Thank God for groups who will still fight for our rights. Will it get worse? The Bible tells of a falling away in II Thessalonians 2:3. I believe it started with my generation in the U.S.A. and it gets worse every generation. And it is not just in America, but worldwide. We may not kill Christians in America (yet), but there are thousands (approximately 16,000) martyred around the world every year. (Allie Martin, OneNewsNow.com 12/31/07). My numbers; that is 44 per day, almost 2 per hour. Just stop and think for moment. Today on your lunch break or Sunday during church, two Christians died for Jesus. What are you willing to do or give? What am I willing to do or give?

We still have the promise(s) of the Word. Remember Romans 8:18; "For I reckon the sufferings of this present time are not worthy to be compared with the glory which shall be revealed in us".

Chapter Six

God Is Still In Charge

**Key verse: … I have written your
name on my hand. Isaiah 49:16 (NLT)**

Some may wonder if the above is still true. Is God still in charge? With all the unrest in our society, from financial worries to social concerns to wars that will not end. I have seen more than one American flag flown upside down, my own included. Not as a sign of defiance, but as an international sign of distress. (If you are military, you will understand. If not military, then you may want to do a little research). This country, as my generation has known it, is certainly in deep trouble. The Supreme Court making sin legal does not make it any less a sin! What is even more important though is our personal relationship with God through Jesus Christ.

I have heard pastors say, "The most awesome characteristic of God is NOT the fact He created the universe and even named the stars (Psalm 147:4). The most awesome characteristic about God is He has a loving, caring, personal relationship with us as Christians (Isaiah 49:15,16 and John 3:16). My name, your name is written on the hand of God (Isaiah 49:16). Luke tells us our names are written in Heaven, chapter 10 verse20. We are written in The Book of Life, Philippians 4:3. One of my former pastors, Brother

Davidson had a favorite saying, "If that doesn't light your fire, your wood is all wet!!" I do believe that would apply here.

God knows us before He forms us in the womb. (Jeremiah 1:5). He has a perfect plan for us, (Jeremiah 29:11) which includes thoughts of peace and not of evil, that will give us an "expected" (planned) end (future). I know I have tested God's plan. I know I have long since gone past plan "A". Probably all the way to plan "Z". Yes, we will fall, but praise God, the Lord will hold us up with His hand (Psalm 37:24). Yes, God has a plan for us, for me, for you.

Even though our thoughts are not His thoughts, Isaiah 55:8, God has a plan. Where is our focus? On Heaven? On this world? See Matthew 6:33, 34. Jude verse 24 tells us He is able to keep us from falling and is able to present us faultless. We are confirmed that we may be *blameless* in the day of our Lord Jesus, I Corinthians 1:8. We are sealed by the Holy Spirit, Ephesians 1;13. We are sealed (by the Holy Spirit) unto the day of redemption, Ephesians 4:30. We are sanctified through Jesus, Hebrews 10:10. We are perfected, Hebrews 10:14. Our sins are not just forgiven, they are forgotten, Hebrews 8:12. There will be no condemnation there. How did all of this occur? Through the blood of Jesus. We will be saved, I Corinthians 3:13-15. So you see, God is in charge.

John says we will be raised up and have everlasting life. We are free. John8:31,32,36. We are redeemed, we are His. Isaiah 43:1. Isaiah 43:2 is part of a song... "Some through the water, some through the flood, some through the fire, all through the blood." Philippians 4:13 tells us we can "do all things through Christ." Verse 19 promises God will supply all our need. The battle is the Lords, I Samuel 17:47. The battle is not ours, but God's, II Chronicles 20:15. Yes, God is in charge.

Proverbs 3:5 and 6 tells us to trust in the Lord. Do I (we) *really* do that? My answer, "sometimes". Your answer?? Or is it only when there is absolutely nothing else left that I can do? WHY?? Why do I even try? Oh, Heaven help me. God forgive me. The Bible is full of promises. I have listed only a few. God **_IS_** in charge. The battle is NOT mine. IF I will just give it to Him. Many of the promises are tied to "If". When things were not going well, Habakkuk rejoiced in the Lord anyway, chapter 3 verse 18. In sorrow, in the face of death, Job chose to trust in the Lord, Job 13:15.

Three of my children have been in the military. Two were deployed to Iraq. My wife and I definitely "caught up on our prayer life" with our children in harms way. Our communication while they were deployed usually was something other than the war itself. Interestingly I received an email from my son shortly after he arrived in Iraq and he had found a Bible study on his base in just a few days. The stories that followed were not so much about the war, but about how God was moving and working in Iraq. How Iraqi soldiers were coming to Jesus Christ as Lord and Savior. Yes, God is in charge.

I love gospel music. My voice is awful and I can't even clap and keep time to the music. But I love gospel music and the message it has. My dad's favorite song was Amazing Grace. My mother's favorite song was I'll Fly Away. I must have a dozen or two favorite songs, maybe more. I would be hard pressed to name just one, but it would most likely be one of those two … or maybe The Eye of the Storm … or maybe the chorus to Just As I Am. Point is, it is often difficult to choose a favorite. The list of songs is endless. There is a story behind each song from the person who wrote the song and those who claim it as a favorite. I came up with a story using song titles. See if you can relate:

This is My Story, that God offers Amazing Grace through Jesus Christ. Some Glad Morning, I'll Fly Away and it will be What a Meeting in the Air. What a Day That Will Be when we get to Beulah Land. This World is not My Home, so When We All Get to Heaven because we have Victory in Jesus, I'll Meet You in the Morning in My Brand New Home which is Just Over in the Glory Land as we pass through The Eastern Gate. All of this because I'm Just a Sinner Saved by Grace because of One Drop of Blood, At Calvary. I know this is not grammatically correct, but to me and my heart it is spiritually correct and for that reason It IS Well With My Soul.

When my kids were teenagers they often listened to Christian Rock. That was quite the challenge for me, but I did survive and so did they. Many churches have gone to what my cousin Johnny calls 7-11 music … 7 words, 11 times, plastered on the wall. My wife, Mary, prefers contemporary Christian music. I still prefer Southern Gospel and will go to my grave with that preference. I have mellowed a bit and after several years, we do agree on several songs. Gospel music incorporates many different ideas. One commentary from a church music leader insisted "his" church learn one new chorus or song every week. I will share a portion of my personal reaction … I would not attend "his" church because it is not "his" church, it is "HIS" church. I am not against learning new songs and choruses … just not every week I go to church!

My mom and dad sang from a hymnal with shaped notes. They seldom used the book as they knew the words and music without any book. We made several trips between Wichita, Kansas and Fayetteville, Arkansas when I was growing up and the singing of mother and dad is still a pleasant memory some 60+ years later. My idea of worship is probably twofold and as different as night and day. One is gospel music and a church with an open alter. The other is camping with my kids on the crick bank, under the stars. How many ways are there to get close to or to worship God? More than one for sure.

So, all we need to do is sing a few songs, praise God, pray a little and life is good – God will fix everything!? Well, maybe not. We must be very careful. I enjoy and collect "one liners", such as "Don't be so open minded your brains fall out", or "You can't soar with eagles when you quack with the ducks". The point is, we all may find comfort in different ways when faced with adversity or uncertainty. Just be careful of those "claiming" to preach the word. We are told to prove all things, I Thessalonians 5:21. How? By scripture:

Jesus warned of unsound doctrine; Matthew 7:21-23.
We are warned again in II Timothy 4:2-5
And yet another warning in I Peter 5:8

Job had the answer; "Though they slay me, yet will I trust in Him", chapter 13, verse 15. If we trust in God and "... seek Him while He is near … ", (Isaiah 55:6), then God will supply all our need as promised in Philippians 4:19. Did you notice the warning in Isaiah 55:6? … seek Him while He is near … implies there are times when God may not be near.

Will leave that for you to decide what you think may be the cause of God not being near. My thought: anytime we are NOT walking the path He has for us.

"The real test of being in the presence of God is, you either forget about yourself altogether or you see yourself as a small, dirty object." C.S. Lewis, Mere Christianity, pg 124. Isaiah 64:6 puts it this way: all our righteousnesses are as filthy rags. (KJV).

No matter how big (cattle on a thousand hills) or how intimate (our names are on His palm), God is in charge.

I own the cattle on a thousand hills. Psalm 50:10 (NLT)

Chapter Seven

Hinderances To Prayer And Healing

Key Verses: James 4:2,3 … "ye have not because ye ask not. Ye ask and receive not, because ye ask amiss, that you may consume it upon your lusts." (KJV)

We will explore several key verses throughout this chapter, several of which will be a "review", although the verses from James above do not leave much doubt.

What is God's purpose for us? Why are we here? Ecclesiastes 12:13 says "Fear God and keep His commandments; for this is the whole duty of man." Deuteronomy 10:12 asks, then answers the question; "... what doth the Lord thy God require of thee, but to fear the Lord thy God, to walk in all His ways and to love Him and serve the Lord thy God with all thy heart and all thy soul..." Micah 6:8 asks and answers "... what doth the Lord require of thee, but to do justly and love mercy and to walk humbly with thy God." You see, God has a plan for us. His thoughts from Jeremiah 29:11 are "... thoughts if peace and not of evil, to give you an expected end."

That is all Old Testament. So then, let's look at the New Testament: I Corinthians 10:31, "Whether therefore ye eat or drink, or whatever ye do, do all to the glory of God." Colossians

3:17 says "And whatsoever ye do in word or deed, do all in the name of the Lord Jesus. These verses apply to our everyday life, our jobs, everything we do. So, do we do this? We can go back to James for more. James has a one sentence introduction and then he gets right to the point. Chapter 1, verse 2, we are to count it joy when we are tempted (tested). Verse 3, the trying of our faith works patience. I have lost count of the number of times I have fallen flat on my face with either one of those! Verse 12, still chapter 1, does help. "Blessed is the man that endureth temptation; for when he is tried, he shall receive the crown of life..." So, here we are again. We are to expect temptation and testing. And, we are to count it joy! Anyone who tells you any different, it is a lie. NOT my opinion, but the scripture just quoted. How do we get through all of these trials and temptations? Prayer and fasting, Mathew 17:21. The verse just before that, verse 20, says if we have faith as a grain of mustard seed, we can move mountains. How? Prayer and fasting. SO, how many of us practice that on a regular basis?

Another form of temptation does not and cannot bring any kind of joy or reward. Still in James, chapter 1, verse 14: "But every man is tempted when he is drawn away of his own lust and enticed." How do you or how can you (or I) expect God to answer prayer when we are not in His will? We should be asking for wisdom, James chapter 1, verse 5 and we should ask in faith, verse 6, expecting an answer. But we MUST be in HIS WILL. Jonah cried out to the Lord and the Lord heard him and delivered him, Jonah chapter 2, verse 2. But what got Jonah in the belly of the great fish in the first place? Disobedience. Chapter 1, verse 3.

The key verses in James 4:2,3 explain much related to our prayer life. We (I) ask and receive not because we (I) ask for "stuff", things, or to get out of a mess, problem or crisis. And, it is often something I caused myself! (much like Jonah). Jeremiah 2:17 asks the question, "Hast thou not procured this (evil) unto thyself ..." Pastor, Evangelist Dwayne Stone put it this way. "We live from spiritual thunderstorm to spiritual thunderstorm. What we need is a total saturation of the Holy Spirit."

However, we need to be very careful. Malachi 2:17 warns of insincerity. "Ye have wearied me with your words ..." Jesus speaking (Sermon on the Mount), Matthew 6:1, "... do not your alms before men, to be seen of them, otherwise ye have no reward of your Father…" verse 4, "… that thine alms be in secret …" verse 7, "When ye pray, use not vain repetition as the heathen do …" Have you ever listened to some people pray and almost every other word is Lord, God, or Father … over and over and over …

Our prayers may go unanswered for many reasons from wrong motives (James 4:3), to unbelief or lack of faith (Matthew 17:20), to unconfessed sin (James 5:16), to insincere prayer (Matthew 6:7). Or, the answer may well be "no". That is not the same as unanswered. Although we many see it as unanswered. We need to be very careful in our discernment. Or, in my case, God may be sitting up there laughing and saying, "Roberts, you have to be kidding!!" (I don't think I am ever going to get that Corvette!! LOL) :) Seriously though, what are we to do if our prayers go unanswered? Well, the Bible addresses our prayer life with some helps.

God already knows our every need. Matthew 6:8, (Jesus speaking), "… your Father knoweth what things ye have need of before ye ask Him…" Verse 32, "… for your Heavenly Father knoweth that ye have need of these things." So, _whatever_ it is we _need,_ God already knows. Key word, "NEED".

Verse 33 goes on to tell us to seek first the Kingdom of God and His righteousness and then all these things will be added. It is ok to ask for what we need or even to give thanks and praise that we have received what we need, but we need to first be seeking the Kingdom.

As for healing. James gives specific directions for healing. Chapter 5, verse 14, "Is any sick among you? Let him call for the elders of the church; let them pray over him, anointing him with oil in the name of the Lord." Verse 15 tells us the prayer of faith will heal the sick and the Lord will raise him up. Verse 16 tells us to confess our faults one to another and pray for one another that we may be healed. "The effectual, fervent prayer of a righteous man availeth much."

You cannot get more specific than how James laid it out. How often do the elders actually get together and actually pray over the sick and actually anoint with oil? It may not always be possible, when it is possible, how often do you see it happen. How often do we offer "fervent prayer"? Author Judy Shelly states "True prayer is not token in a Heavenly vending machine." (Spiritual Care, p39). Remember Matthew 17:20? IF we have faith as a grain of mustard seed, we can move mountains. And how do we get that kind of faith? Prayer and fasting, verse 21. Jesus may or may not have been speaking of a literal, physical mountain. That is not the point. The point is, we all have personal mountains to climb at some point in our life. My wife read of a woman who had been ill for 10 years. She continued to pray all of those years and eventually received healing. What of the woman with the issue of blood for 12 years? (Matthew 9:20, Mark 5:25, Luke 8:43).

I Thessalonians 5:17 tells us to pray without ceasing. Luke 8:1 states we "… ought always to pray…" John 15:7 tells us "If ye abide in me and my words in you, ye shall ask what ye will and it shall be done unto you." That is a promise from Jesus. Why then are our prayers not answered? There is an "if" and an "and". Conditions. Same as II Chronicles7:14. Same as Matthew 17:20, 21. We are warned, "…be not conformed to this world…" (Romans 12:2). Ephesians 6:12 tells us "We wrestle not against flesh and blood, but against principalities, against powers, against the rulers of darkness of the world, against spiritual wickedness in high places." We are struck from all sides, sometimes on a daily basis. The road is narrow and it is often easy to take the wrong path, to backslide and not always be in God's will.

Be thankful we are not in this battle alone. We do have help. I Samuel 17:47 and II Chronicles 20:15 tell us the battle is the Lords. Hebrews 7:25, Jesus lives to make intercession for us. John 17:9 "I Jesus) pray for them … for them which Thou hast given Me; for they are Thine." Jesus Himself, praying to the Father, making intercession for me! (us)!! Romans 8:34 tells us Jesus sits at the right hand of God, making intercession for us. These are powerful verses. Romans 8:26 is also one of the most powerful verses in the Bible. "Likewise the Spirit also helpeth our infirmities: FOR WE KNOW NOT WHAT WE SHOULD PRAY FOR AS WE OUGHT: but THE SPIRIT ITSELF MAKETH INTERCESSION FOR US WITH GROANINGS WHICH CANNOT BE UTTERED." KJV and emphasis mine … We don't even know what to pray for or how to pray. The Holy Spirit intercedes with (effective, fervent, "AGONIZING") groans which cannot be uttered or expressed or put into words … see notes in multiple translations. Remember a few pages back, what my late church sister had to say about the groanings? If satan cannot understand what is being said, he cannot interfere. This is so awesome I can hardly comprehend. Jesus AND the Holy Spirit both interceding to the Father for me!! OH MY!! Once you are saved, there is no way you can ever be "lost" again!

Many times when I do not know exactly how or what to pray, I go to music. Now remember, I cannot clap and keep time to music, without watching my wife Mary. I certainly cannot sing. I do love Christian music, mostly Southern Gospel and old hymns of the church. So, I pray the song to God. I know the Holy Spirit is with and for me, Romans 8:26. And I know Jesus Himself will intercede with and for me, Hebrews 7:25, John 17:9 and Romans 8:34. After that, it is in God's hands. The battle is the Lord's, I Samuel 17:47 and II Chronicles 20:15.

And yes, I know, sometimes things like this are easier said than done. Especially with urgent situations or with wayward children. We have children who have strayed. I have strayed. I have lost track of the number of friends and pastors with children who have fallen away. However, Proverbs 22:6 is a promise from God's Word. "Train up a child in the way he should go; and when he is old he will not depart from it." The challenge is … it does not say how old! I can only imagine the challenges I gave my mother after my father died.

The good news is there is forgiveness for ALL who repent. God can, will and does forgive our sin, I John 1:9. There is more … He not only forgives our sins, He actually forgets our sins, Isaiah 43:25, Hebrews 8:12 and Hebrews 10:17. The challenge I have is forgiving myself. Remember though, Jesus and the Holy Spirit are interceding for me (us).

If you are still bothered by or wonder about forgiveness of your past, here is something from a little book called "Soul Matters for Men", J. Countryman, 2005. If there are past sins that have haunted you and you have truly asked God's forgiveness – Then it is time to move on… write down the thing or things on a sheet of paper. Say a prayer (earnest, serious prayer) and then light the paper on fire and let that symbolize God's act of "scattering your sin as far as the east is from the west. (Psalm 103:12).

Chapter Eight

God Has And We Need An Open Accepting Heart

Key Verse: Revelation 3:20 I stand at the door and knock: "IF" any man hear my voice "and" open the door, I will come in to him and will sup with him and he with me. (emphasis and " " mine).

We all have a story. Life and what has happened to us, life and how we live it. Those whom we may see on a regular basis – family, co-workers, friends – all have a story. Some are happy and you enjoy being with them. Some, well some are not so happy. When you greet them you no longer ask "how are you?" You simply say hello and walk a little faster. Some of the latter are even church going, professing Christians.

One of my favorite sayings used to be, "you can't sore with the eagles when you scratch with the chickens." I have a close friend who collects chickens. Well, my little saying had to change … it is now quack with the ducks! This is the same lady who jolted me out of my "pity party" attitude one morning as I came to work. I don't care how bad her night had been, she always greeted me with a smile and a "how are you". My response was often a sleepy, grumpy, "I'm here." One morning my response was challenged with "I didn't ask where you are, I asked how are you." My response forever changed!!

One Sunday morning a former pastor, Brother Dyer asked the congregation, "If this is day the Lord has made, where is your joy?" I have tried, keep trying, will keep trying. Most days I am successful at "joy in Christ." Some days, I must admit, may seem to others I do not have that joy and I am "quacking with the ducks." But I am trying. I guess I must apologize to those who collect ducks. :) ??

I am a "P.K.". A preacher's kid. I remember when I was in grade school, my parents wanted me to become a "preacher". We lived in Kansas, but came from the hills of Arkansas and daddy was a "Primitive Baptist" minister. I still remember standing behind our huge "over-stuffed" easy chair for a pulpit. (some of you may remember those old chairs – it must have weighed 500 pounds!!??) I am tellin' ya, I could preach hell fire, brimstone and damnation with some of the best!! I even had the "hanky" and would wipe my mouth and the sweat every little while. Well, that just did not work out. Later, I wanted to be a gospel music singer. Mother had a beautiful alto voice and daddy sang bass with the best of 'em!! Me, as I have shared, I cannot clap and keep time to music if my wife is not next to me and I certainly cannot sing.

At age 26, I finally found my calling – EMS (emergency medical service/ambulance tech.). I did not realize my responsibility to God at first, but it did come after awhile. I was a paramedic (in Kansas we were "Mobile Intensive Care Technicians"). Some years later I became a RN and carried both licenses for several years. Today, some 46+ years later, I am retired from health care. I find and then lose at times that feeling of Shalom mentioned earlier (Judy Shelly, Spiritual Care, p21). Shalom refers to both physical health and spiritual health, including salvation and more. As Shelly indicates, Shalom is more than just a word, it is a way of life. Why do so many Christians struggle with peace and happiness … Shalom? Why do I struggle? The suffering I often witnessed in EMS, ER and ICU was usually of a rather short duration, at least on my part of interaction. Still suffering none the less and obviously would stay with the family much longer. The suffering

I would see in long term care (the nursing homes) was just that … long term and often very debilitating. I did feel Shalom when I was able to help "ease" someone into eternity when I knew they would be instantly healed and with Jesus for eternity. I did struggle when I was not so sure of where they were going for eternity. I felt Shalom when I was able to offer them Jesus and they accepted, at a time before they did enter eternity.

For many, the search for happiness or shalom, whatever their definition, is never ending. More money, more power, more sex, more drugs, more whatever. For many Christians, it seems the search either failed or never really began. For some professing Christians, their search is derailed with doctrine which became "… the commandments of men …" See Matthew 15:9, Mark 7:7, Colossians 2:8 and II Timothy 4:3, 4.

We are told in Psalms 34:15 "The eyes of the Lord are upon the righteous and His ears open to their cry." (See also Revelation 3:20). Isaiah 55:6 says "Seek ye the Lord while He may be found…" There may well be times when God in not near and it is most likely because of our own actions. Verse 7 tells us to "… return to Lord … for He will abundantly pardon." Verse 8, "My thoughts are not your thoughts, neither are your ways my ways." Go back to verse 7 again … He will abundantly pardon. We must ask earnestly and sincerely. In Matthew 11:28 Jesus tells us, "Come unto me, all ye that labour and are heavy laden, and I will give you rest." (See Revelation 3:20 – again). See Matthew

17:20 and 21. Something about a grain of mustard seed, moving mountains and prayer and fasting. Sound familiar? John 16:33 tells us we will have tribulation, but Jesus has overcome the world. And He stands at the door and knocks, Revelation 3:20 (again). II Corinthians 1:3, 4, "Blessed be God, the Father of Christ, Father of mercy and God of comfort: who comforts us in All* our tribulation." Remember James 4:2, 3? We do not have because we do not ask. And when we do ask, we ask "amiss". Oh to be humble to the will of God. Remember I John 5:14? If we ask "ANYTHING"* - how? ACCORDING TO HIS WILL*… (*emphasis mine).

Many times throughout scripture we are taught patience. God's timing is not necessarily on schedule with ours. But His is perfect. See Habakkuk 2:1, I will stand upon my watch …

and will watch to see what He will unto me. Verse 4, the just shall live by faith. We can learn from Esther, chapters 4 and 5. She had a plan for deliverance of her people. A plan that could cost her life. But she had a plan and patience. Esther 4:16. Three days of fasting and then she would go before the King. Chapter 5, verse 1, … on the third day … (Esther) stood in the inner court of the King's house (and waited). Verse 2, she obtained favor in the King's sight. Jeremiah 29:11 tells us God has thoughts of peace for us with an expected end .. a plan. We can move mountains with faith by prayer and fasting. (Matthew17:20, 21 {again}, Mark 9:29).

Joni Eareckson Tada (a quadraplegic since a teenager) has, what I believe is an interesting take on suffering. "Reasons why don't ultimately satisfy … Those who suffer are like the hurting child who asks his daddy, "why"? The child opens himself up to the one and only someone who can actually do something about his plight. He knows his pain will be eased by his father's embrace." Our pain too, can be eased by our Father's embrace. Father, God, Yahweh, Abba, "Daddy".

The sports/workout slogan, "No pain, no gain" may also apply to Christian growth. And there is the Marine slogan, "Pain is weakness leaving the body". Our weaknesses leaving to be replaced by God's strengths.

When we do face trials and tribulations, we already have victory. See Psalm 23. II Corinthians 12:9, My grace is sufficient for thee. Hebrews 7:25 and John 17:9, Jesus Himself interceding for us. Romans 8:28, the Holy Spirit interceding for us. The victory is ours. We are free. Romans 8:36, "If the Son therefore shall make you free, ye shall be free indeed." Oh we will face trials and tribulations. But there is a promise. Romans 8:18, "For I reckon that the sufferings of this present time are not worthy to be compared with the glory which shall be revealed in us." A reward we cannot in our wildest thoughts or dreams even imagine. I Corinthians 2:9, "Eye hath not seen nor ear heard, neither have entered into the heart of man, the things which God hath for them that love Him." See also Revelation 3:21.

How often have I made my requests or petitions to God only to start trying to come up with my own answer or solution? Have you ever tried to tell God what He should do? When for another person, another family member, when for salvation for their soul, we must be specific, but we must leave the answer to God. When praying for anyone or anything, I try to be specific but NOT tell God what He should do. A close friend of mine tells me - "if you want to make God laugh, just make plans." So, we must be careful

I have tried personalizing scripture. When I read Isaiah 53:5, I read, He was wounded for Gene's transgressions, He was bruised for my iniquities. The chastisement of Gene's peace was upon Him, and with His stripes I am healed. Or when I read John 3:16, I read, For God so loved Gene Roberts, that He gave His only begotten son, that if Gene believed in Him, Gene would not perish, but would have everlasting life.

Several presidents have turned to God for direction. President Reagan said "If we ever forget we are one nation under God, we will be one nation gone under." Friends, we are headed in that direction at break neck speed!!) President George Bush said "When you turn your heart and life over to Chirst, when you accept Christ as saviour, it changes your heart." President Lincoln once said, "I have been driven many times to my knees by the overwhelming conviction that I had absolutely no other place to go." After 8 years of turning away from God, I believe President Trump is making an effort to bring God back to America once again.

Christians have suffered and died for Christ almost from day one. Christians suffer and die today, world wide. Why should things be any different for you and me? We are blessed to live in this great country for one thing. So we may not have to fear for our lives because of our Christian beliefs, but rest assured, many are being ridiculed and things will get worse. II Timothy 3:1-7 is just one warning of what is to come. However, our promise is eternal life, in His presence. What more could there be? There is a gospel song called "I Have Never Been This Homesick Before". Friends, I am beginning to feel that way myself!

Chapter Nine

Some Things I Still Do Not Understand

Key Verse I Corinthians 1:27 But God hath chosen the foolish things of the world to confound the wise; and God hath chosen the weak things of the world to confould the things which are mighty.

If God knew, and He did, because He is God, then why did He create us, knowing what would happen?

Why did He create Lucifer? Why does God heal some here and some at the "Pearly Gates"? Why is there suffering? Even for children in child prostitution and child abuse, the most horrific of which is abortion. And we keep thinking of new ways to kill them. Partial birth abortion is just one example. Why the Hitler's, why the Sudan's, the Darfur's? The slavery in our own country? The abuse of Native American's? Why did God allow and why did Jesus freely give His life in one of the most brutal deaths ever recorded? Why did it all have to happen that way?

Christianity is so simple a child can understand the need and the way for salvation. Yet, what of theology? Religion is so complicated, no one seems to understand. Religion is much like health care in some ways. The more I learn, the more I realize I don't know. Why so many religions and so many denominations? And even "sub" denominations if you will. Over a dozen Pentacostal already in just over 100 years of formal existance. Over 30 different Baptist denominations. I have been told this by pastors in those respective denominations. Many other denominations have split as well as new denominations have arisen.

Jesus knew what would happen, afterall, He created "everything" that is in the universe. And He knows what is yet to come. Read Matthew chapter 24. Verse 5 tells us many shall come in the name of Chirst, yet they will be deceiving. Verse 7 warns of pestilences, famines and earthquakes. Christians are warned of suffering. Verse 9, believers will be hated and be killed. That has been occuring for centuries although there appears to be a drastic increase over the last several years. Verse 11 tells of false prophets and there appears to be an increase of falsehoods world wide. See I Peter chapter 4, verses 12, 13 and 14 warn us of things to come, but look at what Peter says ... meet this with "exceeding joy". II Thessalonians 2:3 warns of "a falling away" in the end times. Look at the USA since 1973 and since the elections of 2008 and 2012. I believe the falling away (for this country) actually started in the 1960's. We cannot go much lower, what with gay rights, abortion and infantcide. And if homosexuality is right, why did God destroy two cities? One of my former pastors (Bro. Dyer) made the statement, "If God does not deal with America for her sins, He will need to apologize to Sodom and Gomorrah and I do not expect an apology!" And neither do I. We all should know the world has been a mess for a long time, but do you see a trend here? Yes, we could move mountains with faith as a grain of mustard seed. But I have to doubt there was much fasting and praying during the campaign time of 2008 or 2012. When a president commits treason (trading terrorists for a traitor) and when a 2016 candidate that is for killing babies and caused the death of Americans can win the popular vote, I do not see much hope for America. When those claiming to be Chirstian cast an evil ballot three times in a row, I do not see much hope for America. There is much that I do not understand, but according to the Bible, it will happen and is happening.

Matthew chapter 5 also warns of persecution. There is however the promise. Blessed are they which are persecuted, verse 10. Blessed are you when men revile you and persecute you, verse 11. We are told in verse 12, "Rejoice and be exceeding glad: for great is your (our) reward in Heaven." Oh what a promise. See Romans 8:18 (again). We cannot compare our suffering to our coming glory. The promise from Psalm 30:5 is still true today. Joy will come in the morning. Heaven is beyond our (my) wildest dreams, I Corinthians 2:9. Heaven will be worth anything we face down here. I will just say (again), we in America do not know (yet) what suffering for Christ is all about. Do I look forward to that possibility? Well, not really. I just hope and pray, if and when the time comes, I have the courage to stand for Christ like so many before me.

So, I may not understand a lot. I do not understand the coming suffering and persecution. I do not understand why Jesus had to die the cruel death on the cross. We have been warned. Several warnings from the apostles and from Jesus Himself. So, it will happen. That I do not doubt for one second. And this I do believe: Man creates his own adversity, even his own destiny. From Adam and Eve until today, "we" have had choices and it seems "we" have almost always made the wrong choice(s). The good news is, God is still in charge!! Pastor Ken Davidson often said "The good news is, the bad news is all wrong." That is true … IF you know Jesus as Lord and Savior. Heaven is waiting and in the end all of my questions and or doubts will not matter. Yes, I wonder. Yes, there are many things I do not understand. When I reflect on those thoughts and those things I have written, in the end, it will not matter. In fact, I believe we will not remember this life on earth. PTL!! See Isaiah 65:17. "Behold, I will create new heavens and a new earth. The former things will not be remembered, nor will they come to mind." (NIV) As I mellow a bit with the "maturing process" (aging), I ponder these things less and less. From my grandson's death to many in my family having cancer … God is still in charge and if He calls tonight, I just know I will be in the presence of Jesus and all will be well.

As I mentioned a few pages back, when I personalize scripture it often brings a much more personal realization of just what the scripture is saying. When I read John 3:16 that way, it does make me wonder just how could God and Jesus love me so much? Well, I don't often ask that anymore. The fact is, He did and that is good enough for me. I guess I do still wonder at times, especially when I fail in some way. (Still a much too frequent occurrance). If I did ask, it is doubtful I would understand anyway as we know God's ways are not our ways, Isaiah 55:9. And in the end, when we are with Jesus, it really will not matter.

Chapter Ten

My Journey

Key Verses: Romans 8:26 The Holy Spirit is intervening for us (me) with *groanings* which cannot be uttered.

John 17:9 Jesus is praying for me.

Hebrews 7:25 Jesus is making intercession for us (me).

This book is not about me, my story or my journey. This book is about the power of Jesus Christ and how He can change our life, IF we just give it all to Him. My journey is most likely pretty mild compared to many of you. I have had a few bumps in the road, maybe even a few craters! There is an old John Denver song called "Some Days Are Diamnonds, Some Days Are Stones". That sort of fits my 70+ years on this ol' planet. I could throw in another descriptive and say some days are boulders!! But then I would be quacking! Most of us ride the roller coaster of life and most of us "get by". I believe God wants more for us than to just get by. Remember Jeremiah 29:11? God has a plan for us. And I mentioned I have probably taken Him from "Plan A" to "Plan Z". When we mess up, then yes, our life and the "plan" must change accordingly.

I am a P.K., a preacher's kid. My Dad was a Primitive Baptist minister, in the hills of Arkansas, in the 1940's. We were finally allowed to see our first movie when Old Yeller came out. We were finally allowed to play the Old Maids card game, because it was not "really cards". Yes, we were pretty conservative. Many of those same values are still in my life and in my heart. I pray that will NEVER change... ever. And at 70+ years of age, change is not very likely.

My father died in 1962, of cancer, shortly after he turned 59. I had just had my 15th birthday and was a freshman in high school. My mother was obviously pretty devastated. She was a homemaker, unable to work outside the home due to a horrific auto accident some years prior. I turned into a pretty wild teenager and I am sure I added more than a few gray hairs to her head. My older brother was married and lived in another town several miles away. I am sure I added more than a little stress to his life. I was married at 17, a father at 18 and had two children by age 20. I finished high school (P.T.L.) at Mulvane High School, in a small town just south of Wichita, Kansas. I was going to class in the morning and working second shift at what was then Beech Aircraft, in Wichita. After high school, I started college at Wichita State. I was going to be an Industrial Arts teacher and a football coach. My home life was not anywhere close to what it should have been. Oh, we went to church and my wife and I were both (professing) Christians, but God was not the head of our household. Shortly after our second son was born, I took a "high paying" job overseas for a year and a half and later transferred to a location where our family could be together. That did not last long and our marriage ended in divorce. My (ex)wife and children returned to Kansas and I stayed overseas and drifted even farther away from God.

After a year or so, I returned to Kansas and quite by accident, I became involved with my brother who was operating an ambulance service in El Dorado, Kansas. As I look back, it was no accident or coincidence. God had a hand in it, I just did not realize it at the time. I became more involved in what then became "Emergency Medical Services". I took the very first EMT (Emergency Medical Technician) class in the state of Kansas. I eventually became certified as an "Emergency Mobile Intensive Care Technician" (EMICT) or what some call a Paramedic. This was something I really loved doing and eventually became director of a paramedic service in Winfield, Kansas. I had remarried by then and we soon started a "second" family. My wife, Mary and I were both Christians and through serveral different friends and circumstances, we both "re-dedicated" our lives to Jesus. We began to live a more Christian oriented lifestyle. It was somewhere during this time that things started coming together for me. I began to realize my "job" was actually a ministry to God. My wife became an EMT and we were actually able to work together and make ambulance calls together.

Some years later, tragedy struck our family again. Our first grandchild lived only 36 hours before a heart defect took his life. Pastor Davidson was awesome. He read all the right verses. The promise of Jari (pronounced Yari) being with Jesus and our eventual reunion. All in all, it did little to ease my pain. Some 30+ years later and 11 grandchildren later, I often find it difficult to tell folks about Jari.

The pain remains. A challenge we face every year is our twins share his birthday, so we celebrate but we also remember the one we lost.

A few years later, my brother was diagnosed with cancer. Another rude awakening of life to mortality and the challenges to be faced. Mitch had surgery and radiation and was cancer free for 15+ years. His cancer treatments caused some very challenging side effects and he had many struggles for all of those years.

"Next" on the list, one of my girls, Jenna had joined the Army shortly after her marriage. She had completed basic training and was stationed in South Carolina. Her husband, still in Kansas, died tragically. She was able to come home on emergency leave. The Army did allow her that privilege. She did eventually obtain a medical discharge and had some real challenges working through what had happened.

It would be my turn next. A few years after my brother, I was diagnosed with cancer. I honestly did not experience the panic or terror many cancer patients talk about when diagnosed. It was almost as if it had finally happened. My dad at age 59, my brother in his mid 50's and now me at age 55. I think my reaction was more like, OK Lord, this one REALLY IS ALL YOURS. I cannot do anything about this. I have 3 children still in high school and one in college. I really do not have time to deal with this. My family depends on me. So, here is yet another bump in the road. Well, maybe this time it was more like a crater! But we made it. With God's help, a loving wife and supportive family, we made it. 17 years later, I am still cancer free.

Our next challenge was even more devastating to me than my cancer diagnosis. This time is was my wife and the diagnosis was again cancer. For those who have been there, I believe you will agree, it is more devastating when a loved one is the "victim". Following surgery, chemo and radiation, she whipped it, only to have cancer again 14 years later. Surgery and chemo – she whipped it again!! I don't know why she had this cross to bear twice, but God has healed her both times! P.T.L.

Cancer finally did win out with my brother. At age 73, the cancer returned. Due to some very poor medical care, the cancer metastasized to his lungs and bones before being diagnosed. The good news is … he is with Mom and Dad and Jesus. And he is cancer free!!

Many of us will lean on Jesus and in more than one way. Sometimes our leaning turns to bargaining while trying to get the answer or response we want. (Guilty!!) Instead, we need to learn to allow Him to carry us through whatever it is we face. I am often reminded of the poem "Footprints" where Jesus carries us when we need Him most. I recently saw a cartoon about the footprints poem. Could be me!

Yes, my brother, Mary and I all went to doctors and through a cancer treatment protocol. I have been in healthcare for over 47 years and I have yet to heal anyone as a paramedic or a nurse. I hope I have had some small part in the healing process. I have prayed for patients and even for procedures. Praying for a positve outcome. Sometimes praying for something as simple as a blood draw or a difficult IV start. We still pray for complicated treatments or procedures. We have treatment protocols for almost everything in healthcare and most of the time we are pretty proficient. Some patients go home to family, some go into eternity. God still has the final say and we are just His tools. So, looking back over 45+ years of healthcare … I can see when, where and why God put me in various positions and even though it took a "little while" to realize, healthcare both as a paramedic and a nurse was a ministry for me. Not "just a job". I still see folks in town who remember me caring for them and tell me how much they still appreciate the care they received. All I can say is "thank you Jesus".

The reason for this book: To provide a short, to the point reference to help those in need. From the beginning, to meet God and Jesus, if you did not already know them. To the end, with peace, true Shalom with Yeshua and Yahweh. My journey, pretty tame … still some bumps and the need to trust.

I trust the Bible references have been helpful. You may have verses of your own that are more meaningful. I simply chose a few that have been and remain helpful to me. A scripture search of your own may well be the best medicine there is for you and for your challenge. As I mentioned, years ago I stopped having problems. I do still have challenges. Think about it. There is a difference.

Ultimately the answer to your challenge lies with each of you on an individual basis. Between you and God through Jesus Christ. Books are great. Books are sometimes helpful. But give me THE BOOK, not someone's opinion. The intent of this book was to rely on scripture, not my opinion.

Just one last thought …some people create their own storms and then get mad when it rains.

Selected references and suggested readings:
Praying the Names of God … Ann Spangler
Spiritual Care … Judith Shelly
Christian Care Giving … Kenneth Haugk
Called to Care … Shelly and Miller
Why … Ann Graham Lotz
Mere Christianity … C.S. Lewis
When You Are Going Through Hell, Keep Going … Doug Giles
When Your Rope Breaks … Graham, Sittser, Tada … Zonderman, 2009

And of course, THE BOOK … the BIBLE (most quotes, references, unless otherwised noted, are from the King James Version, Scofield Reference Bible, Oxford University Press.) Other versions: NASB (New Amercian Standard), NIV (New International Version) NLT (New Living Translation).

Printed in the United States
By Bookmasters